Sexless Relationship Advice

Cured and Fixed

Table of Contents

INTRODUCTION

Many people suffer from a sexless relationship; you are by no means on your own. Loneliness and bitterness are probably the only two emotions circulating around the marital home at this moment. This problem is usually associated with revenge; one of the partners feels as though they are not receiving the attention they deserve.

Today's society and culture place too much emphasis on the sexual side of any relationship. What one person classes as a problem within the relationship may not even concern other couples, different couple have different priorities.

Discussing the problem openly and honestly between the two of you can be the best way to a resolution. There will be things said by both parties during the discussions which may seem hurtful; these are better out in the open.

Dealing with the situation together will work another way too; it will save you thousands of dollars which you would spend on therapy sessions. Don't get me wrong I am not saying that therapy can't help, for some people whose issues are very deep routed it may be their only choice.

If you feel that you have acted soon enough to prevent the problems of a sexless relationship from escalating, you should try working it out together. This will cause your resolution to feel more satisfying and may help your relationship become stronger. Anything a married couple does together to solve a problem affirms their love and devotion to one another.

There are many couples having this problem. With that in mind, if you're going through this problem you know you're not alone. The most common causes of a sexless relationship are having the same boring routine day after day, physical inability to be aroused, and psychological issues.

Also, loss of interest or attraction to your partner, having a big fight with your partner, and an affair are all other reasons for a sexless relationship. It's not easy to live in a relationship without sex, and it's especially hard for the partner who still craves sex to deal with rejection, confusion, and fear.

To fix this kind of relationship you have to first keep communication constant with you and your partner. You have do this because it helps your partner talk about why and how they are feeling about not having sex. Without communication, there's no relationship, not to mention sex.

Relationships tend to get stale due the fact of a day after day routine. With that said, do something to introduce excitement in your relationship.

Your partner may want you to try something new, and if you're not willing to try this may cause resentment, thus a sexless relationship. Another way to fix this kind of relationship is to do things that don't force sex on your partner.

You could give your partner a back rub, or a foot rub. Do things that help your partner want to be more intimate with you. If the problem in the relationship is deeper, then sit down and talk to your partner about the problems you both feel are in the relationship.

Once you both can identify those problems, you then make promises and commitments to each other to meet each other halfway and fix those problems together.

When you do this, don't worry there will so much sexual tension between you and your partner that it'll be hard for the two of you to keep your hands off each other. This is great sexless relationship help for you.

You can resolve a sexless relationship with hard work and determination. Remember, if you want something enough you can succeed, this goes with many things in life, not just a relationship.

As long as you can see that a problem exists you can start to work on the cause, being distant and avoiding the situation will only make things worse. If you truly are in love with the person you married then there is no subject and no problem that you can't discuss.

For your sake, I've packaged this eye-opening, jaw dropping GUIDE to help you learn about the cures and solutions to your sexless relationship.

What are you waiting for?

LET'S GET STARTED!

CHAPTER 1
SEXLESS RELATIONSHIPS

There are so many taboo subjects and a "sexless relationship" seems to have been added to this growing list. Many people find that talking about their marital problems is an admission of failure.

The truth is that marital problems are on the increase; this may be due to a various number of reasons. The fact remain, there are two people involved in a relationship so it stands to reason that both parties will need help.

Do you remember when the problems first started? This is a good way to finding a resolution. Without knowing the cause of a problem you could be missing the point altogether, this is only going to escalate the situation.

Many marital problems are work related, by this I mean the amount of time one or both spouses spend at work. If one partner goes to work every day and is gone for 10 or 12 hours, this gives their husband of wife time to become lonely. Being lonely then manifests itself to the fact that they feel left out or ignored.

When was the last time you spent quality time together? I don't mean exchanging pleasantries over breakfast or an evening meal. Quality time is classed as times together when both of you feel a common bond; this can be achieved in the some very easy ways.

Think back to before you were married, what used to make your partner happy? Chances are that it wasn't spending every second of every day together; it was probably doing something together which you enjoyed.

A Sexless Relationship doesn't just happen overnight; there is a buildup, usually a breakdown in communication. All of these problems could have been dealt with in the early stages, if you can talk about and admit that there is a problem. Once a problem has got a hold of any relationship, the longer it is there the harder it is to resolve.

If you fail to address the issues which caused the sexless relationship in the first place then you are looking at a very long and lonely relationship which will inevitably lead to some serious counselling and most probably divorce.

You are willing to put aside some time to discuss the issues and work through it together you will be able to bring the love back and save your relationship. It may seem like a lot of work at times, but if you truly love each other than this will be well worth the effort.

A sexless relationship can be hard to overcome, with the right attitude and the best help; you will get through it together. Relationship is the joining of two people, so it takes two people to make it work and also two people to solve any and all problems.

Don't bottle up your problems, if you need help then admit it, even if it's only admitting it to yourself you'll be half way there.

Sexless Relationship can be repaired, but only when the root of the problem is addressed by both people. This is not a problem which will just go away by itself, it needs to be worked on together. If your partner refuses to discuss the problem, start by reminding them of how good things used to be.

CHAPTER 2
WHAT CAUSES SEXLESS RELATIONSHIPS?

Sexless relationship are on the rise throughout the world. The statistics state that around 15% of married couples in the United States alone live in a sexless relationship. This means that they are having sex less than 10 times a year. It's not known whether this is a new phenomenon or whether people are just more willing to talk about it these days.

This is a major problem which threatens the stability of many relationship and also produces a great deal of frustration and loneliness for millions of people. But what causes sexless relationship? Why do they happen in the first place?

When a relationship is sexless due to the consent of both partners, it is a healthy relationship; there are no feelings of resentment or lack of self-esteem. If the lack of sex in a relationship is due to a lowered sex drive by one of the partners then there is a problem and the relationship can be unhealthy.

If your partner is the one with no desire to have intercourse, then you need to decide if you can stay with them and be happy in your relationship with very little sex. If you cannot be content with your relationship in its current state, then you need to decide how you are going to change things.

If your spouse is willing to work with you and make things better, then it is probably in your best interest to take this route. If your husband or wife is not willing to work through the problem, your final decision may have to be separation.

If you are the reason your relationship is sexless, the solution to the problem may be ☐uite different. Think about why you no longer have the desire for intercourse.

Are you having the desire to have sex with other people and not your spouse or is your sex drive pretty dead all together? If the problem is your spouse alone, then you want to take a look at what is causing it.

Do you resent or feel anger towards your husband or wife for something? Are you bored with the typical timeline of things in the bedroom? Are you just plain stressed out? Once you find the underlying cause of the problem, you can work towards a solution.

There are many reasons. In this chapter, I'll try to specify a few of the most common ones:

1. Reduction in sex drive - This is rare but it does happen. Either the man or the woman suffers some sort of physical reduction is sex drive. This can often be treated medically. Again, this is very rare.

2. Lack of sexual attraction - In certain cases, lack of sexual attraction causes sexless relationship and relationships. This happens when one of the spouses lets himself (or herself) go.

Gaining weight, lack of working out or personal grooming, may lead to a decrease in sexual attraction and fre□uency of intercourse, but this is usually just an excuse because there are millions of overweight people who enjoy a healthy and fulfilling sex life. The real reason is usually much deeper.

3. Boring routine and lack of communication - This is the true reason why most sexless relationship occur. The lack of sex is simply a symptom of a relationship gone sour. Usually, the love is still there but the thrill and excitement is long gone.

main problem many couples have is that they fall into an unhealthy and boring routine inside the bedroom and outside. This can kill desire as sexual excitement needs diversification. The key is to get the excitement back into your life.

CHAPTER 3
WHY A SEXLESS RELATIONSHIP CAN LEAD TO DIVORCE?

Understanding why a sexless relationship can lead to divorce can help couples struggling with this issue. When you first realize that intimacy happens a lot less frequently than it used to within your relationship you may come up with viable excuses.

Things like being tired from tending to the kids or having to get to bed early because you have a big day tomorrow all make sense in the short term.

However, when months pass and there is no intimacy at all, that's an entirely different matter. Ignoring a sexless relationship won't remedy it. Understanding the seriousness of the situation is often enough to light a fire beneath the couple because they finally realize exactly what's at stake.

The reason why a sexless relationship can lead to divorce is actually very simple. Physical intimacy is a natural extension of emotional intimacy in a relationship. When one goes missing, the other follows suit.

You and your spouse may not recognize the distance between the two of you initially. But over time when sex isn't part of the relationship any longer, feelings will start to change. The person who always has the excuse for why they don't want to make love may begin to feel their partner resents them.

They likely do, for good reason. Whenever a person feels that their spouse isn't interested in them sexually anymore they start to view them differently and bitterness is just one small part of that along with anger, disappointment and frustration.

Once this happens, the relationship itself is bound to suffer. The lack of intimacy can lead to additional problems outside the bedroom. A small and somewhat insignificant disagreement can become major because the spouse who wants to make love will use any excuse to lash out at their partner.

This obviously leads to more conflict. This typically escalates until it reaches a point where neither person wants to spend time with the other anymore.

Separate bedrooms become the norm and the couple stops talking about anything important. They bottle their feelings up inside and slowly and painfully fall out of love with each other until nothing is left but a shell of the former, loving and passionate relationship. Divorce is the only course of action left to take by then.

A sexless relationship is a serious issue and should be dealt with promptly. If you are living in a relationship in which sex as disappeared, work on improving that now before it's too late for your relationship.

Specific things you say and do can encourage natural responses within your spouse that make them crave to be intimate with you. Saying or doing the wrong thing will only worsen the problem and can lead to your partner feeling emotionally detached from you. Find out what you need to be doing to help your spouse regain their desire for you.

Most couples struggle with discussing the issue of a sexless relationship and as a result, nothing ever changes and both become more and more frustrated. Don't waste another day wishing your intimate life was more fulfilling, change it now.

CHAPTER 4
WHY MEN DON'T WANT SEX IN RELATIONSHIPS?

If you are a woman living in a sexless relationship I am sure that you are trying to figure out why men don't want sex with their wives.

After all, men are supposed to have insatiable appetites for sex, right? So why on earth would a man refuse to be intimate with his wife especially when she's doing everything she can think of to spark his desire.

The truth is however, that even though we've all grown up being given the impression that men are lustful, sex-hungry animals that really isn't exactly the case. Men's sex drives, particularly when they're older than fifteen and in a serious relationship, is much more complex than just being hormone driven.

There are a lot of factors that affect why men don't want sex, and they can range from work related stress, to exhaustion, and to side effects of medications they may be on. But even if those deterrents are there, a man who has a close and loving relationship with his wife will still be intimate and physically affectionate with her, even if sexual intercourse is a problem.

The fact is, that the main reason why men don't want to have sex with their wives is that something has come between them in their relationship.

Men are not just interested physically when it comes to sex. The emotional aspect of lovemaking is very powerful and important to them. Most men have graduated from the teenage "horny" stage where they want to hop in the sack with anything that wears a skirt and moves. Instead, they need to feel a strong emotional connection in order to be interested in making love.

The first step to fixing a sexless relationship and getting your husband interested in making love again is to figure out where in your relationship the two of you started to drift apart, and to work on coming closer emotionally.

You need to make sure you have a clear understanding of sexless relationship. There is so much confusion and misinformation out there about what a sexless relationship means, why they happen, and how you should go about changing them that many women don't even know where to begin.

CHAPTER 5
WHAT TO DO IN A SEXLESS RELATIONSHIP?

If you are in a "sexless" relationship with a partner who does not see this as a problem and you feel this is important to you, you need to talk to your partner about it now.

1. Have you told your partner that this is a problem? It is your responsibility to speak up.

Speaking up is the beginning and possibility of change. Unless you speak up there is no changing this situation. We are often afraid to say anything because instinctively we know that if we do, the status □uo - as we know it - can never be the same.

2. Stop rationalizing and pretending it is okay if it is not.

There is nothing worse than pretending; it is a denial of the Self and all that it stands for. Pretending sends a message to the inner Self that says, "I am not worth it".

3. You are entitled to want sex and physical intimacy in your life even though your partner does not.

It is always a mistake to deny your feelings. Regardless of the outcome, you are entitled to have this important component in your relationship. Physical intimacy is what makes your feel soft and open towards your partner. It is the feeling you need to have in order to want to "make-up".

4. Does your partner continue to ignore your needs even after you have said this is important to you?

This is a very important point. No one can ignore your needs unless you ignore them. It is your job to take responsibility for the things you need and to make sure you are being heard and understood. If you keep saying the same thing and nothing changes, it is up to you to change the dynamic in the relationship.

5. Do you want to stay in a relationship where your needs are not being met?

If the answer is no, this means you need to set a boundary, i.e., a new course of action if nothing changes. Never give an ultimatum. An ultimatum is a threat. A boundary is not a threat, but simply a statement that says how you feel and what you need in order to go forward.

CHAPTER 6
HOW TO GET MORE ROMANTIC IN SEXLESS RELATIONSHIPS

In the beginning of a relationship things are so fresh and unpredictable. The best part about it is developing and exploring feelings and emotions with one another. Every minute and second counts, you feel like you are going to combust if you do not see each other too soon. It's a craving you can't get under control.

The appetite and bond for each other is so strong it's the best feeling you've ever experienced in your life. Love or nothing is the case at this point. The sex is so hot, explicit and so crazy addictive. No one can satisfy you better, you dare to think of another person, you think with so much passion the feeling will last forever.

Then as the relationship get older the fire suddenly subsides and the bedroom with is so cold that you can see your breath! Man what to do now? I call this the hell storm of the relationship, because the sex is still there somewhere, but you have to go through the storm to get to it back on track.

A sexless couple can ruin the bond between one another. So many things can cause the love life to die like stress, being overworked, medications, medical conditions, alcohol, infidelity etc. Whatever ever the case hopefully if you want you can get it back with the right moves form the heart.

Having a healthy appetite for sex is so important in order to keep the relationship alive. Great intimacy can give you energy, help you shed a few pounds, relieve harmful stress and so on and so on. Expressing love with one another is such a beautiful thing when a commitment is involved.

What goes on in the bedroom should never be boring, it should be explored and fulfilling. It just puts the Hancock on everything about a relationship besides trust. How to have better sex should always be a train of thought, if not then you are less likely to participate. "I'm I right"?

Here are some creative, hot and sensual ways to renew your sexual desire: Take a hot and steamy shower together, there is nothing like two wet naked bodies rubbing together in water, with all of the emotions stirring up it so sensual and relaxing it is sure to end just the way you like. Be careful though it could get slippery.

Make plans to go own a romantic getaway. Nothing like going to an exotic beach to get you in the mood. A different atmosphere can really put some naughty thoughts into your head. Naughty can be so fun! Be adventurous explore some adult sex toy websites. Adam & Eve.com is a very popular one.

You never know what wild side may come out when you browse around adult sites. It can change your whole perspective about sexuality. Try being sexy about it, get a more exotic perfume or put on some eye popping and jaw dropping lingerie.

Show a little more skin, if it is one thing men love besides filling up their bellies it's the skin and scent of a woman. By the way add a little lap dance for the entertainment, shake what your mama gave you! Same goes for you guys too, it does not hurt for you to be more creative, it's a two way street.

Touching, kissing, stroking, rubbing etc., Showing feelings physically is a turn on, a touch can go a long way. Take the time to explore each other's bodies. Learn what areas of the body makes your partner more aroused. Study each other I guarantee you'll love it. Sexual health makes it so much more enjoyable.

Communication is just as important as great sex. It is very crucial you know each other's needs and wants. Talk! I know that you've been together for a while and it seems you already know each other, but there are always some issues to be talked about that you thought were cool. Be more understanding to each other's feelings.

Surprise your lover with gifts and special occasions. Make time for a night for just the two of you, lay in the bed in your birthday suit and where a sign that says "I'm hot for you" By flowers, give a full body massage with some oil with some aromatherapy candles in the room to get you more in the mood, make it fun and different etc.

For example; a candlelight dinner in the nude is a start. Might not be for everyone though, "I'm laughing right now", it was just a thought.

Rekindle the romance by revisiting an old favorite spot you two use to love, like a restaurant, the beach or even a skating ring. Fun activities is a open door for passion to emerge. It can make you realize the reason you two are still together. Recognizing your partner's character is five stars.

Expressing your love and devotion may be all that is needed to get things started. If you think you might need a little more too boost your sexual desire, there are female and male enhancements that are safe and very effective at giving you your love life back. Last but not least spontaneity, it can be an adrenaline rush and it can be so fulfilling.

Try some new sex positions and sex games with your lovemaking. It just adds more spice into the bedroom. Sex shouldn't be boring, it should add a burst of energy and light into the relationship, so have fun explore and you can never have enough of it. Well, sometimes you may need a break, but not for long.

CHAPTER 7
WORKING OUT YOUR DIFFERENCES

Remember the days when you and your spouse could hardly wait to fall into bed together to engage in mind-blowing sex? Is it still like that for the two of you, or has some of the magic disappeared leaving you in a sexless relationship? Sexless can be defined as having sex anything less than ten times per year.

Maybe you haven't reached a point like this in your relationship, but it's good to know that as many as 15% of all relationship end up in this predicament. Becoming trapped in a sexless relationship can give both partners feelings of inade☐uacy and frustration, so it's a situation that's best avoided, and can be if you know what you're doing.

The first thing you need to understand is why you and your spouse are no longer interested in intimate relations. Are you fighting so much that you are never in the mood? Has there been a breakdown in communication between the two of you?

Do you find yourself feeling bored with your current relationship and thinking about something more exciting, or is the stress in your life is leaving you too worn out to consider initiating sex with your partner? Problems can be both physical and emotional, and you need to sort out what's causing your particular problems before you'll be able to find a fix.

Which partner is it that no longer has an interest in sexual relations? It's imperative that you figure it out, because intimacy is an integral part of a successful relationship. Men and women are interested in sex for different reasons. Men are very visually-oriented, getting excited by what they see.

Women, on the other hand, are all about feelings, and it's necessary for them to feel happy and loving towards their spouse before they are interested in going any further. A husband who wants a close, loving relationship with his wife needs to be aware of this.

A man who yells at his wife and then thinks that having sex will make things right again doesn't understand the way women operate very well.

Wives, you need to work at looking your best for your husband. No, you don't have to dress up in heels and pearls to impress him, but you do need to look reasonably attractive if you want to spark his interest. This is incentive for women to keep in shape so that they will remain visually appealing to their mates.

In addition, a man needs to feel that he is the most important person in his wife's universe. If children and other people and activities tend to come between you, he's not going to feel as amorous as he once might have.

You can trace all of your sexual problems back to the time when you were both madly in love and totally into each other. Over the years other demands on your time and energy have begun to intrude which can make you forget to focus on your relationship as central to your lives.

CHAPTER 8
SOLVING YOUR INTIMACY ISSUES

There are numerous intimacy issues in a sexless relationship and sometimes it is hard for a married couple to address these problems.

Walking around day after day without confronting the problems can only make the situation worse and eventually push the two individuals away from each other because we are all human and can only take but so much. I am sure you would be extremely surprised to find how many couples allow this very issue to

I am sure that you would be extremely surprised to find out how many couples allow this very issue to break up their once happy homes. If you were to do research, you would find that intimacy issues in a sexless relationship happens to be one of the single most causes of relationship failure. Yes, a lack of affection and intimacy can ruin the very foundation that your union was built on.

While most couples agree that intimacy was not the reason they married in the first place, they still say that it plays a major part in their relationship and they equally value the connection that it represents within their relationship.

No, it is not all about sex. Intimacy encompasses more than sex. When your husband or wife kisses the palm of your hand, rubs your back, passionately kisses you out of nowhere, sends you flowers at work without reason and lays you down and makes love to you for hours; all of this is intimacy.

Intimacy has many levels and is best defined by you. Your definition of intimacy may be very different than mine but that is quite alright, to each his own.

What kind of excuses are you feeding each other? Is work getting the best of you? Are the children always running around the house, never leaving time for the two of you to be alone? Are you just too tired? Are you not in the mood? Are you still in mourning over the loss of a loved one?

Often times things that are bothering us seem to get the best of us, not allowing for any sense of adoration or consideration for others but when you are married you have to overcome this selfishness.

Think about your spouse and how they are feeling; do you honestly feel that you are honoring your marital vows? I am not telling you to disregard your feelings but you have taken very sacred vows and are expected to uphold them.

Have you recently encountered a traumatic experience? Are you depressed? Do you still want to be married? Do you understand the connection that intimacy brings to a relationship? These are all questions that you need to ask yourself to find out what the problem may be or if you already know, bring your issues to the table.

Your wife or husband needs to understand the cause of the lack of intimacy within your relationship. They love you and only want you to be happy inside of your relationship; so you need to pick the best time to have a talk with them.

Intimacy issues in a sexless relationship can drive a husband or wife to do things outside of their character.

Depending on how important sex is to the individual, they may consider looking for comfort outside of the home; which can initially be used as a temporary solution to the problem and turn out to be something more permanent down the line. What about substance abuse?

Sometimes when people feel lonely and as though they have no one to turn to, they turn to alcohol or drugs to console them; not all relationships will encounter this issue but it is definitely a possibility, especially when the person has a history with an addiction.

Giving your wife or husband a little affection even when you don't want to will not kill you. Everyone needs to be held, touched or shown that they are cared for every once in a while especially when there isn't any sex taken place within the home.

CHAPTER 9

HOW TO RESTORE SEXUAL LIBIDO IN YOUR RELATIONSHIP

Try and access yourself to see if you are having any of the following symptoms-

(a) You have sex maybe 10-12 times in 3 years

(b) She has little or no interest in sex and any other sexual activities

(c) Sex becomes a chore for her

(d) You initiate almost all sexual activities

(e) When she does initiate it, she wants to quickly get over with it

(f) You no longer have any sexual fantasies about your partner

(g) You do not feel connected to each other emotionally and sexually

(h) You increasingly feel lonely, dissatisfied, unloved and empty

If you have one or more of the above symptoms, you are likely to face the situation of a low or no-sex relationship or sexless relationship. There may be many underlying reasons for a woman to be not interested in sex and it is very normal for you to feel frustrated when you have unmet expectations.

Here are a few suggestions that you can try at least to start the ball rolling in order to reverse this trend of decreasing sexual desire.

(1) Reclaim your sexual side for yourself

Orgasm is a great stress reliever and there is a need for an outlet for your sexual release. A way you can do is to masturbate. This will help to keep your emotions in check if the level of frustration continues to intensify. Do remember that it is your responsibility to keep in touch with your own physical needs.

(2) Touch her in non-sexual ways

Studies have shown that a simple touch can reduce anxiety, lower blood pressure, decrease pain and fear, inhibit loneliness and release endorphins in the brain that not only make us feel loved, but want to give love in return.

Affection and non-sexual touch can build trusts, deepen intimacy and strengthen a relationship. Holding hands, hugging, kissing and gentle massage of the neck, shoulders and back are wonderful ways to show affection without the pressure of sex. You need to break the touch barrier that is happening between the both of you.

(3) Have a heart-to-heart talk

You can put across how you feel to your woman in a non-confrontation way. You can say something like this - "I love you. I feel that something that is important to me is missing in our relationship. I need a more intimate relationship." Then ask her to set aside a time to have the most open and honest conversation about sex that you can ever have with her.

If she says no, ask if she would prefer to do it with the help of trained personnel such as relationship counselor or a sex therapist who is non-judgmental and unbiased.

If she still says no, tell her that being in a sexless relationship is not what you want and you are willing to work with her to make life together better and that you are asking her to be willing to do the same.

During the open and honest conversation there is a need to find out about your woman's sexuality such as whether she ever feels sexy, either alone or with you; whether she can pinpoint anything that happen to her in the past that can cause her to hold back sexually; has she ever masturbated or have an orgasm; any reasons for her for not wanting to have sex.

There is a need on your part to be dedicated and patient enough to help her discover her sexuality, possibly for the first time. You must also be willing to do whatever it takes to let her feel comfortable enough to feel sexual.

You need to tell her that you feel unloved, dissatisfied and empty when being trapped in a low-sex or sexless situation. Explain to her that you are willing to do anything to make sure she will enjoy a sexual relationship with you as much as you will.

If her level of sexual experience is an issue, offer to show her what feels good for you. Also ask her to show you what feels good to her, the better if she is willing to masturbate in front of you.

Help her to embrace her sexuality and encourage her to share it with you. Learning how to love and please each other is a great bonding experience which can help to strengthen a relationship.

CHAPTER 10
SEXLESS RELATIONSHIP ADVICE FOR MEN

The amount of sex that a couple desires and is comfortable with varies. Some couples have sex weekly, others make love daily and many others' sexual frequency falls somewhere in between that. Yet other couples have sex once a month or once every couple of months.

There is no magic formula that links a specific number of times a couple has sex with the health of their love relationship or relationship.

In general, a sexless relationship is considered to be when a couple who has no sex or has not had sex for several months. Experts stress that you and your mate need to decide what you want when it comes to lovemaking frequency and that it is possible for a couple to choose not to have sex and still maintain a healthy relationship.

However, if you are and your partner are not having sex at all or not having sex with any fre☐uency and this is not okay with you, the term "sexless relationship" may feel painfully appropriate to what you're living.

What can be done if you're in a sexless relationship?

First off, I'm going to list several things that you can do, but it probably isn't going to improve your situation...

• Complain

• Nag

• Blame

• Guilt-trip

• Pressure

• Give an Ultimatum

None of these responses toward your spouse will probably bring positive changes to your sexless relationship. In fact, they will most likely drive your wife further away. Instead, try this advice.

Identify what's standing in the way of sexual intimacy.

If you want to stay in your relationship and start having sex again with your wife, it's important for you to get out of a blaming mode of thinking, speaking and acting. Get curious about what habits, beliefs and experiences of both you and your woman that may be standing in the way of you two making love regularly.

It could be your busy schedules that just about never overlap. It might be unresolved tensions and conflict between you two that are a constant turn-off. It may be sexual abuse or trauma that either of you experienced in the past that remains unacknowledged or unhealed. There may be health challenges that make sex difficult or unappealing to either of you.

If it seems to you that your woman is the one who is always saying "no" and stopping the two of you from having sex, this might be true in part. It's quite likely that there is some dynamic that you also play a part in that is negatively impacting your intimacy in the bedroom too.

As you get a clearer idea of what is standing in the way of you and your wife regularly making love, brainstorm possible ways to start to dissolve those blocks.

Re-prioritize your lives to make time and energy for lovemaking if you two are always too busy. Seek help from a health care professional if health challenges are going on. Learn strategies and work with a trained professional if either of you is struggling to heal from past abuse.

And, by all means, have the courage to acknowledge the built-up resentments and anger from ongoing or past disagreements and be the first one to take a step toward resolving them.

Above all, if you're going to stay in this relationship, you're going to want to work with instead of against your woman to bring improvements. You two can re-connect as you re-discover sexual intimacy with one another.

Start out slow and make sure that you keep communicating about what feels good, what is comfortable, what is turning you both on (and what is not). Stay open and creative.

There may be different ways that your spouse will be intimate or sexual with you now than she was in the past. Make sure that you are sensitive to her needs and wants as well as honest about your own.

Invite yourself to have fun with this. Focus in on the intimate connections you ARE making with one another, that may or may not be sexual. This can take you closer to having more sex again and closer to one another in the process.

CHAPTER 11
SEXLESS RELATIONSHIP ADVICE FOR WOMEN

As women, when we get married we sometimes do it with stars in our eyes. We believe the foundation of the relationship will stay the way it is for the rest of our lives. That's rarely the case. Once real life sets in including the demands of a job and children the dynamic of the relationship can shift.

One area where the change is often very apparent is in the bedroom. If you are a woman in a sexless relationship you are likely feeling a whole range of emotions and you may even be □uestioning whether staying married is the right thing for you.

Equating intimacy with love is something that women generally do. When our husbands don't want to engage in lovemaking anymore we often take it as a personal rejection. If you are a woman in a sexless relationship you may be □uestioning what you've done to contribute to the situation.

Perhaps you feel that the weight you put on after having children is playing a part, or maybe you are wondering whether your husband has taken on a mistress.

Most men will tell you with all honesty that even if their wives have put on a few pounds since their wedding day, they still find her just as attractive. This is rarely the case for a man's low libido, so if you've been fretting over this, don't.

The other conclusion that women jump to when their husband is sexless is that he's not interested in her because he has a new lover. In many cases when a man is indeed cheating he'll actually be more attentive to his wife's intimate needs. Men do this because they feel guilty and also to □uash any suspicion of adultery occurring.

If you are a woman in a sexless relationship you need to realize that the root cause of your husband's disinterest may be related to several things. If it's not a medical issue than you should pay very close attention to how he reacts when you do initiate lovemaking.

If he says he is too tired or that the mood isn't right you need to read between the lines. He may be trying to tell you that there is something else out of balance in the relationship.

Most men aren't the communicators that women are and as such they often struggle with finding the right way to express how they are feeling. If your husband is experiencing stress because of work or something that is happening between the two of you this may manifest itself in the area of intimacy.

He may feel less connected to you emotionally which translates to him feeling less of an urge to be intimate physically with you. Encouraging him to talk about what may be bothering him can be a great help.

never approach the situation in an accusatory way. Let him know that you love and adore him and that you are willing to help with whatever issues may be troubling him.

Specific things you say and do can encourage natural responses within your spouse that make them crave to be intimate with you. Saying or doing the wrong thing will only worsen the problem and can lead to your partner feeling emotionally detached from you. Find out what you need to be doing to help your spouse regain their desire for you.

Most couples struggle with discussing the issue of a sexless relationship and as a result, nothing ever changes and both become more and more frustrated. Don't waste another day wishing your intimate life was more fulfilling, change it now.

Women that live in a sexless relationship are often in a worse place then men stuck with the same relationship problems because while the frustration, depression and humiliation effect men and women both it is a belief that sexless relationship are usually when the women refuses to have sex.

This leaves women with husbands who will not submit to physical intimacy feeling like they have very little support. A sexless relationship is not a symptom of lack of sexual attraction, putting on a few extra pounds does not diminish the emotive and physical intimacy and attraction you once felt for each other exclusively.

These are usually just symptoms of a deeper issue or issues in a relationship that is fre□uently caused by a lack of communication and a lack of understanding that can get so bad it can play a part in ending a relationship though lack of sex and eventually the connection we call love that is enhanced by this intimacy.

Finding out the root causes of these things can be difficult when dealing with men because of their general reluctance to talk of their feelings and open up about their problems and secrets.

A certain amount of patience and understanding must be kept despite your frustrations to delve into his emotive state that will drive his physical desires just as they do for women.

The best bit of sexless relationship advice you can receive is that no relationships is the same and your case while similar to others is uni□ue and re□uires your own touch to fix it, the other bit of advice is to be careful when taking an active hand in trying to solve this relationship problem because the wrong approach can drive your husband further away rather than closer.

CHAPTER 12
SEXLESS RELATIONSHIP ADVICE FOR THE FRUSTRATED

Living in a sexless relationship can be one of the most frustrating, maddening and depressing things for a man or a woman to go through.

Whether you are married or just in a committed relationship sexual compatibility is the glue that binds things tightly and when there is a mismatch in sexual desire it flows into many other aspects of the relationship as well.

To overcome a sexless relationship like this and match up the libidos of both partners there are a few things you can and should be doing.

End Resentment

It is amazing how two people who can love each other so much can keep grudges for so long. Sometimes these resentments are actually unknown even to your partner but are part of a festering feeling of discontentment they might not be able to understand or explain.

Uncovering the causes of these niggles and problems in a relationship then solving them is essential for unlocking the passion again. Both men and women do not feel attracted to their partners when there is that mental blockage which flows through to physical attraction.

Break Out of the Routine

Another passion killer is routine. We all fall into them, we all have them, and most of the time we need routine to order our lives. However, being stuck in a routine that does not encourage love, intimacy and sexuality happens to so many relationships!

Take some simple steps to break out of these routines and do things differently. Be spontaneous and try new things like dancing or camping or even just eating at different restaurants than you used to.

All these new things will build new memories and break the monotony as well as expand your interests together. Once your partner feels free of the constraints of the routine they can start to feel excitement and passion once more.

Talk Beyond the Usual

Communication in the end is the key to warming up a cold relationship. A sexless relationship can be mended and be full of intimacy once more if you know how to talk properly to each other and express the things that are needed to be expressed

However it is not so easy as to jump straight into that. You probably have already talked about this to some degree and have hit a wall of resistance or sheer confusion. This is why all the other points and working on your own self-image are vital to rekindling desire once more but it all ends with communication in words, and also action.

Sexless relationship may seem like the loneliest thing on Earth even though around 15% of married couples live in such a relationship. The reality of sexless relationship is shockingly common. Living in a sexless relationship is an unhappy situation.

If you want to have sex with your spouse more often, you have to start investing time and energy in fixing the problem. Once you start showing your spouse that you're serious about bringing the passion back to your bedroom, you will surely see the rewards.

Showing this to your spouse can have many forms. You can book a vacation together. You can join a tango class together. You can buy a small romantic gift. You can go on a long walk after dinner.

Taking care of yourself is a key to get your spouse to notice you sexually. You can buy new outfits or find a daring hairdresser. If you have noticed the extra pounds you gained, there is a good chance your spouse has noticed them as well.

Do something about that even if it means joining a gym and start a diet. Don't worry, you can do this. Whatever the reason may be, it is in your power to transform your relationship and get the passion back.

CHAPTER 13
CURE FOR A SEXLESS RELATIONSHIP

Many more couples have sex much less fre□uently than at least one partner and often both partners - would like. The problem is that for most couples the passion in their relationship tends to wane with time. They become bored with the relationship and just don't have the feelings for them they once did.

The other reason can be that other pressures, such as career, children and financial pressures, can put sex, and even the relationship, well down on the list of priorities.

If you are in a sexless relationship or would like your sex life to be better, the first step is to realize that it is possible to have a passion-filled relationship or relationship, even if you have been with your partner or spouse for months or even years.

This is true because there are indeed long-term couples not many unfortunately who do have amazing relationships. They love being with each other and are crazy about each other. They have passionate sex lives which gets better with time. And they seem to be exceptionally happy and alive in each other's company.

If it's possible for other couples in similar circumstances to yourself then it's certainly possible for you. You just need to work out what they do and do it - because the truth is the whole underlying dynamics of their relationship are very different to those of "average" couples.

So what are they doing differently? Well the most important thing to realize is that they have a set of beliefs that keep each other at the center of each other's lives. Think back to when you and your partner first fell in love. Didn't you just think they were the most amazing, beautiful, exciting, sexy person on the planet?

And let me ask you - do you still feel that way? If the answer is no, then you need to restore the beliefs and feelings you had at the start of your relationship. This is definitely possible because they are the feelings and beliefs that couples who maintain passionate relationships have.

You may be concerned that, even if you do start to feel that way again, it will be a waste of time because your partner will not share the same passionate feelings as you. But what happens is that when you have these "passionate" beliefs, you begin to act differently in your relationship or relationship.

Once you do that you will influence your partner's beliefs very strongly. Pretty soon you have them believing what you do about the two of you, and their behavior will change as well.

This is not deception or trickery. It comes from a place of very deep love for your partner and is about you putting renewed energy into your relationship. You cannot fake it, and you also cannot change your behavior (and your results) by simple willpower. You must change things at a fundamental level, which is in how you view your relationship or relationship.

Most couples in sexless relationship have simply drifted into that place. They wake up one day feeling regret and realizing that the passion and sex are way below what they would like. They think back fondly to the early days of their relationship or relationship and resign themselves to thinking the passion is gone forever.

Don't do that! Work on your beliefs. Above all, work on changing them back to what they were at the beginning. This is the path to creating a great sexual relationship, one that was even better than it was and one which will keep developing over time.

CHAPTER 14

REKINDLING THE ROMANCE IN YOUR RELATIONSHIP

Sexless relationships are a sad state of affairs. What should be a union of intimacy, passion and love can somehow turn into once of routine and cold sexless beds. Everyone reacts differently to these situations but unfortunately many react badly and over time make the situation worse.

How to survive sexless relationships needs time and effort but the desire you once both felt for each other can return you persist and do the right things such as:

Stop Blaming Yourself

If you still desire your partner then it is not you that has the problem. There may be issues in the relationship but it is not solely your responsibility for their lack of desire. Your body is nearly always not the issue to both men and women so forget that sort of thinking.

There are emotional gaps that are driving you apart that can be solved and some of that needs to come from you finding ways to bridge that gap without forcing the issue.

Change Your Routine

Routine and boredom are one of the biggest passion killers in a relationship. Doing the same thing every day, every week becomes monotonous and this can flow into your sex life. Often partners may feel like they have a flat mate of a brother or sister and not a lover because the relationship appears to be based on just "getting by".

Kids, work, money and other factors can lead to this but they can all be juggled to accommodate some time to be together in a new capacity. Try to pick up new hobbies you can share or new activities and change your current routine around a bit to be more spontaneous and you will go a long way to helping your relationship.

Their Body Issues

Sometimes the problems come from your partners issues with their own body. Embarrassment at how they look or how they feel can lead to some serious mental roadblocks that inhibit passion. Something this can become so bad they feel they do not actually like sex anymore and need to be reminded how attractive they are.

This can sometimes be hard, you can tell them that all the time but they won't believe you because they think you are just trying to be nice. You need to find other ways to boost their confidence as well as just the words.

If you're living in a sexless relationship, you might think that you're destined to live without intimacy for the rest of your married life. This couldn't be further from the truth.

Not only should you try to have a romantic relationship with your spouse, but it's completely possible to move past your dry spell and onto a fulfilling and intimate relationship.

This may seem like the furthest thing from your mind right now but with a few simple steps, you can rekindle the romance in your relationship and fix your sexless relationship.

These steps have more to do with how you two interact than candy, flowers and sexy lingerie. Before getting to all of those things, you need to build some basic emotional bonds between the two of you.

One of the first keys in fixing a sexless relationship is to build trust between you and your spouse. You can't truly be intimate or even romantic with a person if you don't trust them. If you've had an experience in the past with your spouse that has caused you not to trust him or her, you've got to take steps to rebuilding that trust.

In addition to trust, respect is also an important part of the e☐uation. You can show respect for your partner by keeping your private matters private. If you make a habit of talking about your spouse in a negative way to your friends or family members, you have to put a stop to it.

Even if you hide this kind of stuff from your spouse, the attitude comes through in your interactions. When you start showing respect by keeping your thoughts to yourself, your spouse will begin to take notice.

Finally, you need to listen to your spouse. Listening is an ultimate sign of respect and trust. Even if you aren't at the point yet where you can sit down and talk about your lack of intimacy, you can listen during your day to day activities. Take interest in your spouse's day and he or she will begin to open up more.

Of course, this just scratches the surface of what you can do to rekindle the romance in your relationship. Some couples may need more in depth help in moving past infidelity, repairing trust or just heating up the relationship.

CHAPTER 15
GETTING OUT OF A SEXLESS RELATIONSHIP

There are many couples for whom a sexless relationship appears to be perfectly fine (and there may even be medical reasons making sex not possible), but in general a relationship without sex causes stress to one or both of the partners.

After all, we are essentially sexual creatures, and as such sex is one of our most basic (and human) needs and desires. If that need is not being fulfilled then we are not living up to our potential for happiness as human beings.

The first thing you should do is make a decision: Is the lack of sex in my relationship really acceptable and desirable for me? Think forward ten years from now. Do you think you will have missed out on a great deal of joy and intimacy if you continue to deny your sexual needs?

Make the decision that you will (or will not) allow things to carry on as they are and that you will do something about it. Realize that without some action things will never change.

The second thing you should do is decide what to do. Will you leave the relationship? Will you attempt to revive the sexual element of your relationship?

Will you find an alternative outlet for your sexual needs (such as having a lover). If you are not happy with the status quo then these really are the only options you have.

Remember that making any decision will invariably create some pain. I am not saying for a second that it might be anything but extremely difficult to leave a relationship, and that you might have to make some great sacrifices.

However, in thinking through your actions look into the future and imagine a time where things will be much brighter and you will have fulfilling sex as a part of your life. You CAN do it, but of course to achieve it you must be prepared to take some decisive action and see it through.

If you decide to leave your sexless relationship then the third thing you must do is simply: Do it! Many people wait for years for the 'right' moment and the 'right' way to do it. However, there is no 'right' way or time. Your partner will react the way they will react. Hopefully, if they are mature and you inform them of your decision in a calm manner they will cope.

However, you must expect they will be hurt because it will be the end of a life as they know it for them too. Be compassionate but do not waver. Remember, it is your life and you have a responsibility to yourself to be true to yourself and live in a way that will satisfy your happiness. That is not being selfish, it is being real.

In the end the only way to leave a sexless relationship, after you have decided that it is the right decision for you, is simply to do it as □uickly and decisively as possible. And always think forward with optimism to a life filled with love and great sex.

Before leaving a sexless relationship you might decide you'll try to reignite your partner's sexual desire. This is very possible to do.

CHAPTER 16
FIXING A SEXLESS RELATIONSHIP WITH LESS COMMUNICATION

Sexless couples are an anomaly and not the norm in our society. Yet still there is a large proportion of relationship that need help to fix a sexless relationship before it becomes too last and the gap widens so far that divorce and affair and other relationship problems appear and destroy it.

This does not need to be the case however if you are stuck in a sexless relationship because you can take action to bring back intimacy and love with your spouse without you having to be forceful or deceitful or anything nasty at all.

The trick is to work on the things that you can control to prepare the way for your spouse, be it your husband or wife to become warm to the idea of sexual relations once more. With the right attitude and some changes to your lifestyle this can be achieved.

Make sure that you first put aside all the blame and resentment that you may feel. Anger does not solve a thing and blaming your wife or yourself does not achieve a result.

If you focus on what you want and you really want to get it then all the niggles that you want to lash out about are just a petty nuisance compared to your goal. Be clam, be loving, be understanding and you will melt away the barriers that have been thrown up. This paves the way for good communication but more on that later.

The other factor in your control is your home environment. The day to day wear and tear of relationship can take its toll on your libido and some people become sexless couples more from this than anything else. You have the power to shake that up somewhat.

A change of routine and the way you do things coupled with a few exciting or intimate experiences combined with your new attitude will make that crack in your partners sexless demeanor that much wider.

There is a time you should be working to talk about the problems between you and your spouse but before that you need to be comfortable about yourself. This is because all too often when you are desperate and wanting an answer your communication becomes an interrogation.

This can often lead to your partner thinking you are overbearing or weak and in either case you are not attractive to them like this and also you are not really listening to their issues.

A level of self-rediscovery is needed by anyone who has a sexless wife or sexless husband. This means finding out what makes you tick now, your life has changed over time and so have you but do you really know how or why this is?

Taking a step back from your relationship maybe the best way to take two steps forward later as you will have a much clearer view of yourself, your relationship and you will appear stronger and more attractive as a man or a women to your spouse.

Once you feel more confident in yourself when you do open those communication lines you will not fall prey to your own self-doubt or problems because in the end it is your partner who has rejected a healthy intimate relationship not you. This is the person who needs the help and understanding to overcome these issues.

CHAPTER 17

WAYS TO COPE IN A SEXLESS RELATIONSHIP

There are many reasons why a relationship becomes sexless. It can be caused by medical issues, couples became too busy with their careers and jobs, having children, exhaustion, lack of sex drive or desire, etc.

If you decided to stay in a sexless relationship, no matter what the cause of the lack of sex in your relationship, coping with a sexless relationship needs some work.

Choosing to stay in a sexless relationship is a personal choice but it is worth saving your relationship. Can this kind of relationship work? It don't work in every relationship but to others, yes, a sexless relationship works.

There are couples who are in a sexless relationship for years and yet living a happy, meaningful married life because they've learned to cope with a sexless relationship.

Here are some helpful ways to cope with a sexless relationship.

Do not blame yourself or your spouse. The lack of sex in your relationship doesn't mean you are no longer desirable or attractive. There are many reasons behind a sexless relationship and it is an issue that both you and your spouse are involved so it is not entirely your fault.

Do not blame your spouse either because blaming is not the solution to this issue but it will just aggravate the situation. You and your partner are in this together so it is best to face this issue together to find the best solution. It is less challenging to cope with a sexless relationship if you will stop blaming each other.

Have an agreement or compromise. It is important for both partners to talk about the lack of sex in their relationship. It is best if you both agree and decided to live a meaningful and happy married life despite the lack of sex in your relationship.

It is not easy, as you both may encounter trials and challenges while trying to cope with a sexless relationship but what is important is that you communicate about it and be able to find the middle ground, compromise and come out with an agreement. You both have to work hard together than other couples to be able to cope with a sexless relationship.

Explore other ways to stay emotionally and physically connected. Understand that emotional intimacy in a relationship cannot be attained through sexual intercourse only.

Although it may be true that sex is one of the best ways for couples to connect emotionally, the lack of sex doesn't mean your relationship is doomed. There are other ways for spouses to stay emotionally connected.

Lack of sex is not uncommon in a relationship and there are celibate couples who lead a meaningful and happy married life. Stay emotionally and physically connected with each other. Emotional intimacy is not only about sexual intimacy but it is more about matters of the heart.

Emotional connection with each other doesn't always involve your genitals. Explore other ways to stay connected with each other.

Emotional connection can be made by making time for each other, communicating regularly, listening to each other, opening up with each other, doing things together, playing together, creating new hobbies or memories together, taking a vacation or couples retreat together.

Explore other ways to stay physically intimate with each other. Hugging each other more, kissing regularly or massaging your spouse are some ways to stay physically connected with each other.

Work on the issues behind your sexless relationship. There's nothing much you can do if the reason behind your sexless relationship is a medical issue but to accept the reality and try your best to cope with a sexless relationship.

If the reason for the lack of sex in your relationship is something else, it is best to work on the issues together. If it's not a medical issue, what's causing your lack of sex drive?

Is the lack of physical intimacy a result of unresolved marital issues? Is your careers or individual issues causing you to drift apart? Sometimes the lack of sex is not the problem but it is the result of other issues in your relationship.

While you may both consider that it is okay not to have freꞎuent sex with each other, still it is best to work on the underlying issues to make sure that your relationship is okay and there are no unresolved issues.

If you need help to resolve the issues causing your sexless relationship, do not hesitate to seek help. It is best to exhaust all possible solutions to save your relationship.

Focus on the wonderful things your relationship have and not what's lacking in your relationship. It can be more challenging and frustrating to cope with a sexless relationship if you will keep thinking about what is lacking in your relationship so stop being negative and start focusing on the positive side of your relationship.

Sex maybe one important part of a relationship but there are other things in your relationship that you should be grateful and those things may serve as reasons why you should continue loving and respecting your spouse.

Is the lack of sex in your relationship enough reason to leave your relationship? I hope not, because true love must be beyond sex. Dealing with issues in your relationship is not easy but it is always worth saving your relationship.

CONCLUSION

I feel that a sexless relationship is okay if both parties are perfectly content with each other and see nothing wrong with it. The problem arises when one person still has the urge to have sex and the other has totally lost it.

Counseling can fix situations like this, but sometimes the person who does not feel the need to make love may not even want to consider counseling because they feel there is nothing wrong with the way they are.

Lovemaking is one of the deepest ways couples express their love for each other. A lot of times, when either the man or the woman is not getting what they want in bed from their partner, the likelihood that one person will cheat dramatically increases especially if both physical and emotional needs are both not being met.

If you are in this situation and you are considering the possibility of cheating on your mate, don't do it. It is better and more ethical to either work through the issues you have to see if you can fix it.

And when you can't fix it, it may be best that both of you go your separate ways if you feel that there is no way you can live a happy life together without sex. Talk to your mate and see how they feel.

If your lovemaking once curled your toes and all you are getting now (stress) has your stomach in knots, it may be worth finding out from your mate what has happened to ☐uench their lovemaking fire.

If they say their problem is due to the amount of work they have at the office, then tell them to consider lightening their work load and eliminate bringing work home.

However if the problem has arisen because your partner has gained a lot of weight which has made less attractive, then this is something that can be corrected with exercise. If this is the case, then perhaps getting your partner to joining a gym to lose the weight will turn things around for both of you.

Whatever your situation is, as long as both of you are happy with what you have, then you have no problem, ignore the statistics. But if you are not happy because of it, then do something about, but do not cheat on your mate.

BEST WISHES!

THE END

Dear Readers, thank you for spending your precious time to read my books, it was my pleasure to create these books for you. I hope to know more about your feedback on this novel, please spend a few minutes and give me a honest review! Therefore, i could improve and write better contents for you in the near future! Appreciated and have a nice day ahead! God bless!

73373736R00033

Made in the USA
San Bernardino, CA
04 April 2018